PUFFIN BOOKS
UK I USA I Canada I Ireland I Australia
India I New Zealand I South Africa

Puffin Books is part of the Penguin Random House group of companies
whose addresses can be found at global.penguinrandomhouse.com.
www.penguin.co.uk   www.puffin.co.uk   www.ladybird.co.uk

First published 2016
001

Written by Daniel Roy

ACKNOWLEDGEMENTS
The publishers are extremely grateful to OvisAriesBombus, Drazelic, DicemanX, Flors
and BrushStroke (Andrew D. King, STEAM_0:1:45372054) for their kind permission
to reproduce their inspiring Terraria designs in Chapter 9.

Printed in Slovakia

A CIP catalogue record for this book is available from the British Library

ISBN: 978–0–141–36990–7

All correspondence to:
Puffin Books
Penguin Random House Children's
80 Strand, London WC2R 0RL

MIX
Paper from
responsible sources
FSC® C018179

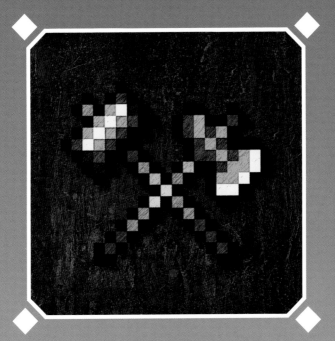

CRAFTING AND CONSTRUCTION HANDBOOK

PUFFIN

INTRODUCTION

Want to become a master craftsman and builder? Let me show you how!

Hello! The Goblin Tinkerer here. Our mutual friend the Guide asked me to teach you the secrets of goblin crafting and engineering. After all, millions of Terraria artisans and builders have used my help to unlock the full potential of their crafts and constructions.

From crafting powerful items like the Frostspark Boots or the cell phone, to building gravity-defying works of art, I wrote this guide so that you, too, can join the ranks of the master craftsmen and builders that have turned Terraria into an art form.

So grab your Work Bench and your toolbelt, it's time to make things!

CONTENTS

From time to time another ally will chime in with a specialized tip of their own. After all, we're here to help! Just build us nice houses and we'll call it even.

CHAPTER ONE: CRAFTING BASICS

CRAFTING ESSENTIALS AND USEFUL TRICKS

Crafting in Terraria is a very simple process with vast possibilities. Before we get to advanced crafting, though, let's review some basics!

CRAFTING CONTROLS

Everything that can be crafted in Terraria, from a torch to the Solar Flare Pickaxe, is done using the Crafting menu. You can access it by pressing Escape at any time.

BEGINNER TIP

New to Terraria? Look for **Terraria: The Ultimate Survival Handbook** at your local bookshop or online retailer! The Guide will take you through the first few days of playing in Terraria and explain the basics you'll need to get crafting and building.

HARDMODE CONTENT

Sections marked with this picture indicate content only available in **Hardmode**. You'll need to defeat the **Wall of Flesh** before you can unlock it, but be careful: your world will become much more difficult as a result.

To select a recipe, either click it in the list on the left, or open the Crafting window and click the item you want there. Review the list of ingredients, and when you're ready, click on the item you want to craft. So easy, even a human can do it!

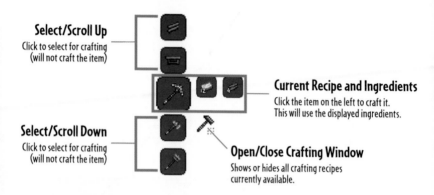

Select/Scroll Up
Click to select for crafting
(will not craft the item)

Current Recipe and Ingredients
Click the item on the left to craft it.
This will use the displayed ingredients.

Select/Scroll Down
Click to select for crafting
(will not craft the item)

Open/Close Crafting Window
Shows or hides all crafting recipes
currently available.

MAN YOUR STATIONS

Except for a few recipes that can be crafted anywhere, creating items in Terraria requires **crafting stations**. There are dozens of crafting stations available in the game. Make sure to stand close to the station you want to use, then open the Crafting menu.

Using the Work Bench

USING THE GUIDE

I may be an expert in goblin crafting, but even I consult our friend the Guide on occasion. If you've ever got an item and you're wondering what you can do with it, just take it to the Guide and ask him.

To use the Guide, simply talk to him. Select **Crafting**, then place the ingredient that interests you in the empty slot. The Guide will give you a list of all the items that you can craft using this ingredient and their recipes, plus the crafting station you'll need for it.

ADVANCED CRAFTING TIPS

SPEED IT UP: QUICK CRAFTING

Want to craft multiple copies of an item in a flash?
Right-click the item in the Crafting menu, and hold
down the mouse button until you reach the number
you want! The speed increases the longer you hold
the button, so make sure to stop before you end up
with a pile of leftovers!

Better stock up on Wooden Platforms

CLOSER TOGETHER: CRAFTING WORKSHOP

It's a good idea to keep your crafting stations close together so you can move quickly
between them as you craft objects. Since crafting stations can be placed on Wooden
Platforms, you can pack them pretty closely together.

Consider dedicating one room in your base to your crafting. Make sure to keep some
shelf space for chests, so you can craft directly from them, or store your extra materials.

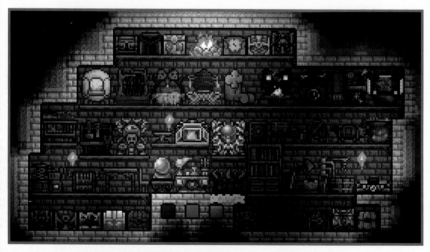

A compact workshop with Hardmode crafting stations

HELPFUL HACK

Notice the **Demon Altar** in that workshop? You can't move altars . . . but
you can build your crafting workshop around one! Connect the workshop
with your base using minecart tracks or a teleporter for quick access.

HOLD THAT THOUGHT: AUTOPAUSE

Need to craft items with monsters jumping around? Turning on **Autopause** will pause the game while the Crafting menu is open. You can turn it on from the Settings menu, under **General**. If Autopause is on, you won't be able to use items directly from your inventory: you'll have to first place them in your Hotbar, then leave the Inventory menu.

MULTIPLAYER TIP

Autopause only works in Single-player mode. There's no way to pause the action when playing with friends, so make sure you're crafting somewhere safe!

CLOSE TO YOUR CHEST: CHEST CRAFTING

Tired of lugging around crafting ingredients? Here's a Tinkerer tip! Set up a **chest** next to your crafting station, and put your ingredients in it! Simply right-click the chest to access its contents, then open the Crafting menu: the list of available recipes will include those that make use of the items in your chest.

Crafting straight from a chest

PORTABLE CHESTS

The **safe** and the **piggy bank** are containers you can carry even when they contain items. They're great places to stock your most common ingredients so they're always on hand. The **Merchant** sells the piggy bank for 1 Gold; you can also buy the safe from him for 20 Gold, but only after you beat **Skeletron**.

If you get a **Money Trough** from a zombie during a **Blood Moon**, you can use it to summon a flying version of the piggy bank!

Here, piggy piggy!

CHAPTER TWO:
CRAFTING STATIONS

CRAFTING STATIONS AND HOW TO GET THEM

A master craftsman is nothing without his crafting stations. Let's get your collection started!

CRAFTING STATION CHECKLIST

BASIC STATIONS

GOT IT?	CRAFTING STATION	USED TO CRAFT ...
✓	By Hand	Basic items
	Work Bench	Various useful items
	Furnace	Bars, materials, glass
	Hellforge	(Hellforge can also craft Hellstone Bars)
	Iron Anvil or Lead Anvil	Tools, weapons, armour (Both have the same functionality)
	Placed Bottle	Potions
	Alchemy Table	(Alchemy Table sometimes doesn't consume an ingredient)
	Sawmill	Furniture
	Loom	Silk and silk-related Vanity items
	Chair + Table	Watches
	Chair + Work Bench	Goggles and sunglasses
	Cooking Pot	Food items
	Cauldron	(Both have the same functionality)
	Tinkerer's Workshop	Combined items with multiple functions
	Imbuing Station	Flasks
	Dye Vat	Dyes and paints
	Demon Altar or Crimson Altar	Boss-summoning items and Night's Edge (Depends on whether your world has Corruption or Crimson)

 **HARDMODE STATIONS**

GOT IT?	CRAFTING STATION	USED TO CRAFT . . .
	Mythril Anvil or Orichalcum Anvil	Tools, weapons, armour (Upgrade from Iron/Lead Anvil)
	Adamantite Forge or Titanium Forge	Bars, Hellstone Bars, Hardmode Bars (Upgrade from Hellforge)
	Bookcase	Hardmode magic weapons
	Crystal Ball	Endless Quiver, Endless Musket Pouch, visual-effects building items
	Autohammer	Shroomite Bars
	Ancient Manipulator	Powerful items from Fragments and Luminite

SPECIALIZED STATIONS

GOT IT?	CRAFTING STATION	USED TO CRAFT . . .
	Keg	Ale
	Heavy Work Bench	Text Statues and special blocks
	Blend-O-Matic	Asphalt Blocks (Hardmode only)
	Meat Grinder	Flesh Blocks (Crimson only, Hardmode only)

LIQUIDS

Liquids can be used to craft simple items such as Bottled Water, but can also be combined with the crystal ball crafting station to create special blocks.

GOT IT?	CRAFTING STATION	USED TO CRAFT . . .
	Water	Bottled Water, Mud Blocks, Waterfall Blocks*, Magic Water Dropper*
	Honey	Bottled Honey, Honeyfall Blocks*, Magic Honey Dropper*
	Lava	Lavafall Blocks*, Magic Lava Dropper*

* When crystal ball nearby.

THEMED FURNITURE

The purpose of these stations is to craft furniture with a unique theme.

GOT IT?	CRAFTING STATION	FURNITURE THEME
	Bone Welder	Bone
	Glass Kiln	Glass (Also functions as a Furnace)
	Honey Dispenser	Honey
	Ice Machine	Ice
	Living Loom	Living Tree
	Sky Mill	Sky
	Solidifier	Slime
	Steampunk Boiler	Steampunk (Hardmode only)
	Flesh Cloning Vat	Flesh (Crimson only, Hardmode only)
	Lihzahrd Furnace	Jungle Temple (Hardmode only)

THE WORK BENCH

A Tinkerer classic, the Work Bench is the most useful crafting station available, and the easiest one to craft. It allows you to craft a great number of items including other crafting stations, blocks, furniture and even some weapons and armour.

RECIPE	INGREDIENTS	CRAFTING STATION
Work Bench (1)	Wood (10)	By Hand

WORK IN STYLE

While almost all other crafting stations have only one possible look, you can change the look of your Work Bench based on what material you use to craft it. You can use everything from cactus to Honey Blocks or bone to craft your own unique Work Bench, so go nuts!

Additionally, there are five Work Benches you can't craft yourself. Four of them can be found in the Dungeon, while the last - the Obsidian Work Bench - can be found in the ruined houses of the Underworld.

WORK BENCH COMBOS

The Work Bench qualifies as a flat surface for the purpose of creating a **Placed Bottle**. By placing a **chair** next to the Work Bench, you can create the **Chair + Work Bench** crafting station, which you can use to craft goggles and sunglasses. We'll get to the Placed Bottle in a moment.

Three stations in one: Work Bench, Placed Bottle, and Chair + Work Bench

THE FURNACE

The furnace's main function is to turn ore into bars. You can also use it to create a number of blocks, as well as some glass-based objects.

RECIPE	INGREDIENTS	CRAFTING STATION
Furnace (1)	Stone Block (20) Wood (4) Torch (3)	Work Bench

HELLFORGE

The Hellforge is an upgrade to the furnace. It works exactly the same way, but also lets you craft **Hellstone Bars**. You can't craft a Hellforge, so you'll have to travel to the Underworld and look in ruined houses for one.

You can use any pickaxe to mine a Hellforge in the Underworld. You can also just destroy the blocks below it and pick it up. Once you place it yourself outside the Underworld, you'll be able to pick it up again with your pickaxe.

A Hellforge in its natural environment

HARDMODE FORGES

Once you reach Hardmode, you'll have access to a new type of forge that can also smelt Hardmode ores. The type you'll get depends on whether your world features **Adamantite** or **Titanium**.

RECIPE	INGREDIENTS	CRAFTING STATION
Adamantite Forge (1)	Adamantite Ore (30) Hellforge (1)	Orichalcum/Mythril Anvil
Titanium Forge (1)	Titanium Ore (30) Hellforge (1)	

THE ANVILS

Anvils in Terraria allow you to craft weapons, armour and tools – so you should try to get your hands on one as soon as possible. Both anvils work in exactly the same way; the only difference is the ore you use to make them.

RECIPE	INGREDIENTS	CRAFTING STATION
🔨 Iron Anvil (1)	Iron Bar (5)	🪑
🔨 Lead Anvil (1)	Lead Bar (5)	Work Bench

BEGINNER TIP

If you don't want to sacrifice 5 bars to craft your anvil, have a word with the **Merchant**: he sells the Iron Anvil for 50 Silver.

HARDMODE ANVILS

In Hardmode, you'll have access to a brand-new anvil to replace your old, banged-up Lead or Iron Anvil. These require **Mythril** or **Orichalcum**, so it'll take some time before you can get them. Don't worry: your old anvil can still forge items from Cobalt and Palladium Bars.

RECIPE	INGREDIENTS	CRAFTING STATION
🔨 Mythril Anvil (1)	Mythril Bar (10)	🔨🔨
🔨 Orichalcum Anvil (1)	Orichalcum Bar (12)	Iron/Lead Anvil

THE PLACED BOTTLE

The Placed Bottle is a special crafting station that lets you craft potions. You can create it by placing a bottle item on a flat surface.

BOTTLES

The following items all qualify as bottles for the purpose of this crafting station:

RECIPE	INGREDIENTS	CRAFTING STATION
Bottle (2)	Glass (1)	Furnace
Pink Vase (1)	Clay Block (4)	Furnace
Wine Glass (1)	Glass (1)	Work Bench
Dynasty Cup (1)	Dynasty Wood (2)	Work Bench
Honey Cup (1)	Honey Block (1)	Honey Dispenser

Another type of cup, the **chalice**, can only be bought from the Traveling Merchant.

SURFACES

Any flat surface will work for placing a bottle. This includes **platforms**, **tables**, **Work Benches**, **dressers**, **pianos**, **bookcases** and even the **Tinkerer's Workshop**.

THE ALCHEMY TABLE

The Alchemy Table is an upgrade from the Placed Bottle. When using it to craft potions, there is a thirty-three per cent chance for each ingredient not to be consumed – which is useful for gaining more value out of your potion ingredients. You can find the Alchemy Table in the Dungeon.

THE SAWMILL

The sawmill is used to craft advanced wood furniture such as **beds**, **dressers**, **pianos** and **bookcases**.

RECIPE	INGREDIENTS	CRAFTING STATION
Sawmill (1)	Wood (10) Iron/Lead Bar (2) Chain (1)	Work Bench

THE LOOM

Using the loom, you can craft **silk** from cobwebs, as well as a number of Vanity items and magical robes.

RECIPE	INGREDIENTS	CRAFTING STATION
Loom (1)	Wood (12)	Sawmill

THE COOKING POT

The purpose of the cooking pot is to cook fish into **Bowls of Soup**, **Cooked Fish**, **Cooked Shrimp** or **Grub Soup**. When you eat these, you'll get a boost to your combat stats.

RECIPE	INGREDIENTS	CRAFTING STATION
Cooking Pot (1)	Iron/Lead Bar (10) Wood (2)	Iron/Lead Anvil

STYLE TIP

On Halloween, the **Witch Doctor** sells a **cauldron**, which works exactly like the cooking pot, but with a more bewitching look!

THE BOOKCASE

You can acquire the bookcase at any point in the game, but once in Hardmode you can use it to craft three powerful magical weapons that use mana for devastating ranged attacks: **Crystal Storm**, **Cursed Flames** and **Golden Shower**. There are twenty-six craftable variations of the bookcase, and six non-craftable ones.

RECIPE	INGREDIENTS	CRAFTING STATION
Bookcase (1)	Wood (20) Book (10)	Sawmill

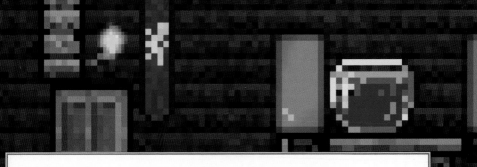

LIQUIDS AND THE CRYSTAL BALL

Water, **honey** and **lava** can all be used to craft special items. You can use them, like any other station, by simply standing next to a pool of the liquid you need.

LIQUIDS AT HOME

If you're tired of running back and forth between your base and the nearest lake, there is a simpler way! Craft an **empty bucket**, collect some water, then make a one-block hole at home and drop the water in it. Do the same for honey and lava and you'll be all set!

RECIPE	INGREDIENTS	CRAFTING STATION
Empty Bucket (1)	Iron/Lead Bar (3)	Iron/Lead Anvil

THE CRYSTAL BALL

The crystal ball can be purchased from the Wizard for 10 Gold. You can use it to make a number of animated blocks, as well as items that provide an endless supply of ammo for your ranged weapons: the **Endless Quiver** and the **Endless Musket Pouch**.

Many of the crystal ball's unique blocks require a liquid nearby. It's best to place your crystal ball near liquid deposits to unlock its full potential.

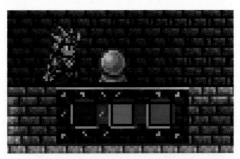

The three liquids with a nearby crystal ball

NON-CRAFTABLE STATIONS

THE EVIL ALTARS

The **Demon Altar** and **Crimson Altar** allow you to craft boss-summoning items. Once you reach Hardmode, you can hit them with the **Pwnhammer** to release Hardmode ores. Make sure to keep one intact for all your crafting needs, though!

CRAFTING TIP

Keep the altar closest to your base intact for crafting purposes. You can build a minecart track to get to it and back, or better yet, a **teleporter**.

THE IMBUING STATION

You can use the Imbuing Station to craft flasks, which give bonuses to your melee weapons. The Witch Doctor sells it for 7 Gold.

THE DYE VAT

The **Dye Vat** is used to create dyes and paints. You can purchase it from the **Dye Trader** for 5 Gold.

THE TINKERER'S WORKSHOP

My own invention, the Tinkerer's Workshop, lets you combine the functionalities of multiple items like a true goblin inventor. You can buy this station from me, the Goblin Tinkerer. Once you've defeated the **Goblin Army**, look for me in underground tunnels. Free me and I'll move into an empty house.

THE AUTOHAMMER

The **Autohammer** allows you to craft **Shroomite Bars**, which you can in turn use to craft a powerful armour set that boosts your ranged attacks. Getting it is a bit tricky, though: you'll need to build a **Glowing Mushroom biome** on the surface of your world, then build a house for my old friend the **Truffle** to move in and sell it to you. The Truffle ally will only show up in Hardmode.

To build a Glowing Mushroom biome, visit a Glowing Mushroom Cave and hit Glowing Mushrooms to gather **Mushroom Grass Seeds**. Then, lay at least 100 **Mud Blocks** on the ground. Plant the Glowing Mushroom Seeds, and give them time to spread to nearby blocks.

Grow, my pretties!

Once the Mushroom Grass has spread to all your Mud Blocks, the area will turn into a Glowing Mushroom biome and the Truffle will move in. Go talk to him to buy the Autohammer for 1 Platinum.

Aaaah . . . Shroom, sweet shroom

THE ANCIENT MANIPULATOR

The **Ancient Manipulator** allows you to craft powerful items from **Lunar Fragments** and **Luminite**. You'll have to beat the **Lunatic Cultist** to get your own. To face the Lunatic Cultist, beat Golem in the Lihzahrd Temple, then kill the cultists that show up at the Dungeon's entrance.

SPECIAL CRAFTING STATIONS

THEMED FURNITURE STATIONS

Here's where to find all the themed furniture stations. These allow you to create cool-looking items with a unique look. See the Furniture Guide section in **Chapter Seven: Building with Style** for details.

CRAFTING STATION	HOW TO GET IT
Bone Welder	Chests in Dungeon
Glass Kiln	Crafted using 18 Iron/Lead Bars and 8 Torches
Honey Dispenser	Ivy Chests in Underground Jungle
Ice Machine	Ice Chests
Living Loom	Living Wood Chests in Living Trees
Sky Mill	Floating Islands
Solidifier	Dropped by King Slime or sold by Steampunker
Steampunk Boiler	Sold by Steampunker after defeating a Mechanical Boss (Hardmode only)
Flesh Cloning Vat	Sold by Steampunker in Crimson worlds (Hardmode only)
Lihzahrd Furnace	Jungle Temple (Hardmode only)

THE KEG

The keg can be used to craft ale, which will give you a combat bonus, but also a small defence penalty!

THE BLEND-O-MATIC

With this crafting station, you can turn Stone Blocks and gel into **Asphalt Blocks** that will greatly increase your movement speed. You can purchase it from the **Steampunker**.

THE MEAT GRINDER

This station is dropped by Herplings, Crimslimes, Floaty Grosses and Crimson Axes in Crimson worlds. You can use it to craft **Flesh Blocks**, which you can then use with the Flesh Cloning Vat to create macabre furniture ... because nothing says 'stylish elegance' like a sofa made from someone's insides.

CHAPTER THREE:
MATERIALS

A GUIDE TO TERRARIA'S MOST USEFUL RESOURCES

Any good recipe needs ingredients. Here's how to find the best ones.

ORES

From tools to weapons and armour, metal ores are the central ingredients of the majority of recipes in Terraria. The more advanced the ore, the more powerful the **pickaxe** you'll need to mine it. Always make sure to upgrade your pickaxe to the most powerful version available!

PICKAXE TYPE	RECIPE	STATION	CAN MINE . . .
Cactus	Cactus (15)	Work Bench	
Copper	Copper Bar (12), Wood (4)		Common ores
Tin	Tin Bar (12), Wood (4)		
Iron	Iron Bar (12), Wood (3)	Lead/Iron Anvil	
Lead	Lead Bar (12), Wood (3)		
Silver	Silver Bar (12), Wood (3)		
Tungsten	Tungsten Bar (12), Wood (4)		Common ores Meteorite
Bone	(Dropped by Undead Miner)		
Candy Cane	(Obtained from presents during Christmas)		Common ores Meteorite Demonite Crimtane
Gold	Gold Bar (12), Wood (4)		
Platinum	Platinum Bar (12), Wood (4)		
Nightmare	Demonite Bar (12) Shadow Scale (6)	Lead/Iron Anvil	All pre-Hardmore blocks
Deathbringer	Crimtane Bar (12) Tissue Sample (6)		
Molten	Hellstone Bar (20)		All pre-Hardmode blocks Cobalt*, Palladium*
Reaver Shark	(Fished from the Ocean)		

* Hardmode-only ores

Once you enter Hardmode and acquire the **Pwnhammer**, you'll be able to smash **Demon Altars** and **Crimson Altars** to spread new types of ore throughout the world. Be careful, though: every time you do so, there's a chance you'll spread the Hallow and either the Corruption or the Crimson, which will quickly contaminate your biomes!

All Hardmode pickaxes and drills can mine every type of pre-Hardmode blocks.

PICKAXE/DRILL TYPE	RECIPE	STATION	CAN MINE ...
Cobalt	Cobalt Bar (15)	Lead/Iron Anvil	Cobalt Palladium Mythril Orichalcum
Palladium	Palladium Bar (18)		
Mythril	Mythril Bar (15)	Mythril/Orichalcum Anvil	Cobalt Palladium Mythril Orichalcum Adamantite Titanium
Orichalcum	Orichalcum Bar (18)		
Adamantite	Adamantite Bar (18)		
Titanium	Titanium Bar (20)		
Pickaxe Axe* Drax*	Hallowed Bar (18) Soul of Might (1) Soul of Sight (1) Soul of Fright (1)		All except Lihzahrd Brick
Chlorophyte	Chlorophyte Bar (18)		
Shroomite Digging Claw*	Shroomite Bar (18)		
Spectre	Spectre Bar (18)		
Picksaw*	(Dropped by Golem)	Ancient Manipulator	All blocks
Solar Flare	Solar Fragment (12) Luminite Bar (10)		
Vortex	Vortex Fragment (12) Luminite Bar (10)		
Nebula	Nebula Fragment (12) Luminite Bar (10)		
Stardust	Stardust Fragment (12) Luminite Bar (10)		
Laser Drill*	(Dropped by flying saucer during Martian Madness event)		
Drill Containment Unit	Luminite Bar (40) Chlorophyte Bar (40) Shroomite Bar (40) Spectre Bar (40) Hellstone Bar (40) Meteorite Bar (40)	Mythril/Orichalcum Anvil	

* Also works as an Axe.

GEMS

There are six types of gems in Terraria: **Amethyst**, **Diamond**, **Ruby**, **Emerald**, **Sapphire** and **Topaz**. You can find gem deposits throughout the Underground and Cavern layers, as well as in rare Gemstone Caves. A seventh type of gem, **Amber**, can be acquired by processing Desert Fossil; see the next section for details.

Gems of all types can be used to craft magic **staffs**, **robes**, **hooks**, **stained glass** and coloured **Gemspark Blocks**.

A small Ruby deposit

You can also use gems to craft **Phaseblades** – futuristic and cool-looking broadswords that emit light when you swing them. All Phaseblades have the same stats, but you can pick your favourite colour by using a different gem type when crafting one.

DESERT FOSSIL AND AMBER

While digging in the Underground Desert you'll eventually run into Desert Fossils. You can place them on an **Extractinator** to produce **Sturdy Fossils**, gems, ores, coins and Amber.

You can find an Extractinator in **Gold Chests**, **Ice Chests** or from fishing **Wooden Crates**. They can also be found in rooms in the Underground Desert. You can use them to process **slush** and **silt** as well, though these yield less Amber.

You can use Amber to craft **Orange Torches**, **Amber Gemspark Blocks**, **Crate Potions** and the **Amber Staff**.

HERBS

Herbs are important components of **potions**. You'll encounter them everywhere you go, but if you need larger quantities, it's also possible to grow them.

To gather herbs, just hit them with any weapon or pickaxe. If the herb is currently in bloom, you will gather **seeds** as well.

HERB (NORMAL/IN BLOOM)	COMMON IN...	GROWS ON...	BLOOMS WHEN?
Blinkroot	Underground	Dirt, Mud	Randomly
Daybloom	Surface	Normal Grass Hallowed Grass*	During the day
Deathweed	Corruption Crimson	Ebonstone, Corrupt Grass Crimstone, Crimson Grass	During Full/Blood Moon
Fireblossom	Underworld	Ash	At sunset
Moonglow	Jungle	Jungle Grass	At night
Shiverthorn	Snow	Snow, Ice	When fully grown
Waterleaf	Desert	Sand, Pearlsand*	When it rains

* Hardmode block

YOUR OWN SECRET GARDEN

Tired of running around looking for herbs? You can use **clay pots** or **planter boxes** to plant seeds. You can craft clay pots yourself, and buy planter boxes from the Dryad.

RECIPE	INGREDIENTS	CRAFTING STATION
Clay Pot (1)	Clay Block (6)	Furnace

GARDENING TIP

The various types of planter boxes are just for decoration: you can plant whichever seed you want in every one of them. For instance, you can plant Moonglow Seeds in a Firebloom Planter Box and your Daybloom Seeds in Moonglow Planter Box.

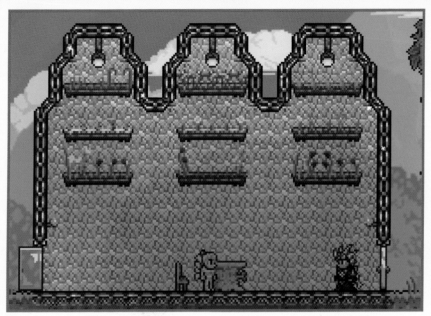

A greenhouse using planter boxes (the lights are purely decorative)

THE STAFF OF REGROWTH

The Staff of Regrowth is a must-have tool for any serious gardener. When you swing it at planter boxes and clay pots, it will only harvest the herbs that are in bloom, while swinging it at herbs on regular blocks will always give you seeds no matter what.

The Staff of Regrowth can also be used to grow **grass** or **moss** on Mud and Stone Blocks. While moss is purely decorative, grass allows you to plant many types of seeds. You can find the Staff of Regrowth in **Jungle Shrines** or in the **Jungle Crates** you can get from fishing in the Jungle.

FISHING ITEMS

Fishing in Terraria is a great way to collect some powerful items. To fish, make sure you have a **fishing pole** and some **bait** in your inventory. Then stand next to a fairly large body of water, and click on it with your fishing pole.

When you see your floater bob, click again to reel it in. Simple!

Aaah . . . So relaxing.

There are a number of factors that will influence the quality of your catches. These include the power rating of your fishing pole and bait, your equipment and potions, the size of the body of water and a few others.

FISH

From potions to hearty meals, there's a lot you can do with your fishing catches. Whenever you catch a new fish, make sure to ask the Guide about what it can be used for.

You can use the most common fish to make **Cooked Fish**, **Cooked Shrimp** and **Sashimi**, all of which will give a boost to your stats when you eat them.

FISHING CRATES

Although rarer than fish, crates are another good reason to cast your line. Each crate you fish contains valuables ranging from coins to rare weapons and items. Crates vary depending on the environment you fish for them in.

FISHING QUESTS

The Angler's fishing quests are a source of many exclusive items such as the **Fisherman's Pocket Guide**, the **weather radio** and the **sextant**, used to craft the cell phone. (See **Chapter Four: Epic Crafts** for details.) The Angler will also give you useful fishing gear including bait, as well as the occasional Gold.

The Angler can give you one fishing quest per day. You have until 4.30 a.m. to return with the fish he requires, otherwise you'll have to start all over again.

FISHING TIP

If you want me to show up, have an empty house ready and look for me near the Ocean. Wake me up and I'll move right in. I promise I won't make up dangerous quests to punish you for interrupting my nap. Hee hee.

METEORITE

A goblin favourite, Meteorite is a special ore you can use to craft powerful armour, weapons and furniture with a sci-fi theme. Meteorite is not available on your world at the start; instead, a meteor has a chance to crash once you've destroyed your first **Shadow Orb** or **Crimson Heart**.

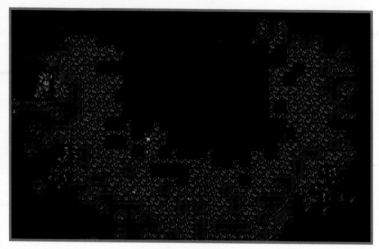

A meteor crash site

MINING METEORITE

You'll need a Tungsten Pickaxe or better to mine Meteorite.

Meteorite Blocks burn to the touch, so you'll have to proceed with caution to mine them. You'll be all right if you hit them from a distance then pick them up. Just make sure the **Meteor Heads** don't knock you into an ore deposit!

Two useful items to mine Meteorite without burning yourself to a crisp are an **Obsidian Skull** and **Obsidian Potions**. Both will protect you from the Meteorite's burning effect. Another method is to use **dynamite**, **bombs** and **Sticky Bombs** to blow up the Meteorite, then pick it up safely.

RECIPE	INGREDIENTS	CRAFTING STATION
Obsidian Skull (1)	Obsidian (20)	Furnace

RECIPE	INGREDIENTS	CRAFTING STATION
	Bottled Water (1), Fireblossom (1)	

DEMONITE ORE AND SHADOW SCALES

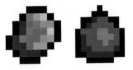

These two resources are only available on worlds featuring Corruption. They are very important if you want to upgrade your weapons, armour and tools.

While Demonite Ore can be found in small quantities underground, the best source is from bosses. Beat the **Eye of Cthulhu** to acquire some and upgrade your weapons.

When you feel confident in your improved weaponry, go and destroy three **Shadow Orbs** to summon the **Eater of Worlds**. Even if you don't defeat it, each segment you destroy will drop some Shadow Scales and Demonite Ore. Use them to craft your very own **Nightmare Pickaxe** and **Shadow Armor**.

CRIMTANE ORE AND TISSUE SAMPLES

Crimtane Ore and **Tissue Samples** work in the exact same way as Demonite Ore and Shadow Scales for Crimson worlds. Once you're ready, head down into the caverns of the Crimson and destroy three **Crimson Hearts** to fight the **Brain of Cthulhu**.

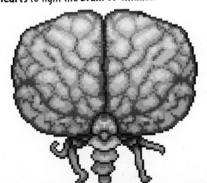

The **Creepers** that protect him will drop Crimtane Ore and Tissue Samples, so even if you don't beat the Brain, you should soon have enough ore to craft the **Deathbringer Pickaxe**.

OBSIDIAN

Obsidian is a special resource required to craft **Hellstone Bars**, along with a lot of other useful objects. You'll need a **Nightmare** or **Deathbringer Pickaxe**, or better, to mine it. If you don't have one, a well-placed **bomb** or **Sticky Bomb** will do the trick as well!

Obsidian is rare: you'll need to create it yourself by arranging for water to come into contact with lava. The easiest way to do this is to dig tunnels down to make water fall into the lava pools of the Cavern or Underworld layers.

HELLSTONE

Hellstone is the most powerful pre-Hardmode resource in Terraria, but it's also very dangerous to mine. Not only is it only found in the monster-filled **Underworld**, but touching blocks will also set you on fire, just like Meteorite. And if that wasn't enough, hitting a block with your pickaxe will leak some lava that can quickly burn you alive!

Who says fire and water don't mix?

The best way to mine Hellstone is to create **Obsidian Skin Potions** that will grant you immunity to lava. Just head to the Underworld, gulp down a potion, and get to work!

RECIPE	INGREDIENTS	CRAFTING STATION
Obsidian Skin Potion (1)	Bottled Water (1), Fireblossom (1) Waterleaf (1), Obsidian (1)	Placed Bottle

SOULS

Souls are a special category of items dropped by enemies in Hardmode. They are used to craft many powerful items that you'll need to defeat **Plantera**, a tough Hardmode boss who lurks in the Underground Jungle.

NAME	DROPPED BY . . .
Soul of Flight	Wyverns in Space
Soul of Light	Monsters in Underground Hallow
Soul of Night	Monsters in Underground Corruption/Crimson
Soul of Might	The Destroyer
Soul of Sight	The Twins
Soul of Fright	Skeletron Prime

HALLOWED BARS

Hallowed Bars are special bars that can't be mined. Instead, you can get them by defeating one of the three Mechanical Bosses: **The Destroyer**, **the Twins** and **Skeletron Prime**. Each drop the same quantity, so pick the easiest one for you and beat some Hallowed Bars out of it!

Hallowed Bars are used to craft powerful items such as the **Hallowed Armor** and **Excalibur**. You can also use it to craft the **Pickaxe Axe** (or its drill equivalent, Drax) – the first pickaxe that lets you mine **Chlorophyte**.

RECIPE	INGREDIENTS	CRAFTING STATION
Pickaxe Axe (1)	Hallowed Bar (18) Soul of Might (1) Soul of Sight (1) Soul of Fright (1)	Orichalcum Anvil Mythril Anvil

CHLOROPHYTE ORE

Chlorophyte Ore is one of the most powerful ores in the game. You'll need a **Pickaxe Axe** or better to mine it in the Underground Jungle.

Like other ores, Chlorophyte Ore is an ingredient for more powerful weapons, armour and tools. Combined with **Turtle Shells**, you can craft the powerful **Turtle Armor**, a high-defence set that reflects damage back on to the attacker.

SPECTRE BARS

Spectre Bars are used to create **Spectre Armor**, a powerful armour set that boosts your magic abilities. To craft Spectre Bars from Chlorophyte Bars, you'll need **Ectoplasm**, an ingredient that drops from the Dungeon Spirit after you defeat Plantera.

RECIPE	INGREDIENTS	CRAFTING STATION
Spectre Bar (2)	Chlorophyte Bar (2) Ectoplasm (1)	Titanium Forge Adamantite Forge

There are two types of head armour for the Spectre Armor set: the **Spectre Mask** boosts your magical attacks, while the **Spectre Hood** heals and protects you.

SHROOMITE BARS

Shroomite Bars are used to craft **Shroomite Armor**, a great armour set that boosts your ranged attacks. You can also craft the powerful **Shroomite Digging Claw**, the fastest pickaxe tool in the game. You can craft a Shroomite Bar by combining a Chlorophyte Bar and Glowing Mushrooms.

RECIPE	INGREDIENTS	CRAFTING STATION
Shroomite Bar (1)	Chlorophyte Bar (1) Glowing Mushroom (15)	Autohammer

The catch? You'll need an **Autohammer**, which you can only get from the **Truffle**. See the Autohammer section in **Chapter Two: Crafting Stations**.

FRAGMENTS AND LUMINITE

These super-advanced crafting materials allow you to craft the most powerful and awe-inspiring items in the whole of Terraria. Each kind of Fragment lets you craft a type of armour that helps in one specific type of combat.

FRAGMENT TYPE	ARMOUR BENEFIT
Solar Fragment	Enhances melee protection
Vortex Fragment	Increases ranged damage
Nebula Fragment	Boosts magic damage
Stardust Fragment	Summons powerful guardian

Fragments are only available once you defeat Golem in the Jungle Temple. Kill the cultists gathered at the entrance of the Dungeon, then defeat their leader, the **Lunatic Cultist**. Once you beat him, four pillars will appear in your world: destroy them to gather the Fragments.

As for Luminite, you'll have to defeat the ultimate boss of Terraria: the terrifying **Moon Lord** himself!

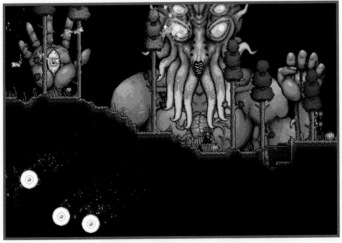

AAARGH! I take it back!! You can keep your Luminite!

CHAPTER FOUR: EPIC CRAFTS

ADVANCED CRAFTING RECIPES

Want to put your crafting skills to the test? Here are some of the most amazing items and weapons in Terraria!

FROSTSPARK BOOTS

These marvels of goblin engineering will speed up your movement, steady your footing on ice and even let you fly by jumping a second time in mid-air. The items are rare and will take some time to hunt down, but you'll still be wearing your trusty **Frostspark Boots** deep into Hardmode.

SHOPPING LIST

Except for my ingenious Rocket Boots, which I'll sell you for 5 Gold, you'll need to look in **chests** around the world to find the ingredients you'll need.

ITEM		WHERE TO FIND IT
🥾	Rocket Boots	Sold by Goblin Tinkerer
🥾	Hermes Boots*	Chests (Underground and Jungle)
🥾	Flurry Boots*	Ice Chests (Underground Snow)
🥾	Sailfish Boots*	Wooden and Iron Crates (fishing)
🔘	Anklet of the Wind	Shrines (Underground Jungle), Jungle Crates (from fishing)
▬	Aglet	Chests (Surface and Underground), Wooden Crates (from fishing)
👟	Ice Skates	Ice Chests (Underground Snow)

* Only one of Hermes Boots, Flurry Boots or Sailfish Boots is required.

CRAFTING FROSTSPARK BOOTS

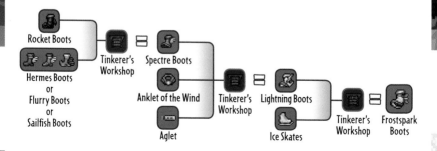

Rocket Boots

Hermes Boots or Flurry Boots or Sailfish Boots → Tinkerer's Workshop = Spectre Boots

Spectre Boots + Anklet of the Wind + Aglet → Tinkerer's Workshop = Lightning Boots

Lightning Boots + Ice Skates → Tinkerer's Workshop = Frostspark Boots

NIGHT'S EDGE

Night's Edge is the most powerful weapon before Hardmode, and a key ingredient in one of the ultimate weapons in the game – the Terra Blade. To craft it, you'll need to combine four legendary weapons: **Fiery Greatsword**, **Blade of Grass**, **Light's Bane** and **Muramasa**.

If your world features the Crimson instead of the Corruption, you can use the **Blood Butcherer** instead of Light's Bane.

SHOPPING LIST

ITEM	WHERE TO FIND IT
Hellstone (60)	Mine (Underworld)
Obsidian (20)	Created when water touches lava
Jungle Spores (12)	Destroy glowing green orbs (Underground Jungle)
Stinger (12)	From hornets and Spiked Jungle Splimes (Underground Jungle)
Muramasa	Gold Chest (Dungeon) Golden Lock Box from Golden Crate (fishing in Dungeon)
Demonite Ore (30) or	Mine (Underground, rare) From Eye of Cthulhu, from Eater of Worlds
Crimtane Ore (30)	Mine (Underground, rare) From Eye of Cthulhu, from Brain of Cthulhu

CRAFTING NIGHT'S EDGE

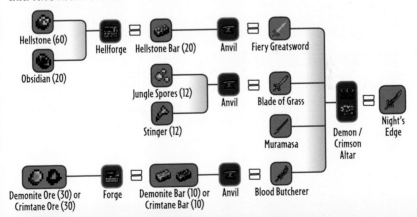

HARDMODE TIP

You'll find much better weapons than Night's Edge once you enter Hardmode, but don't throw away that blade! It's a component in **True Night's Edge** and the **Terra Blade**. See the Terra Blade section of this chapter for details.

ANKH SHIELD

The Ankh Shield is the best defensive item in the game. It provides immunity to eleven types of special afflictions such as Poisoned, Bleeding, Confused, Cursed and Burning, and protects you against knockback as well. Many of the items required are very difficult to find, so be patient, and swap with friends!

SHOPPING LIST

ITEM	WHERE TO FIND IT
Obsidian (20)	Created when water touches lava
Cobalt Shield	Locked Golden Chests in Dungeon, Golden Lock Boxes in Dungeons
Trifold Map	Dropped from clown, mummy or giant bat
Fast Clock	Dropped from mummy, Dark Mummy, wraith or pixie
Vitamins	Dropped from Floaty Gross or Corruptor
Armor Polish	Dropped from Armored Skeleton or Blue Armored Bones
Blindfold	Drom from Dark Mummy, Slimeling or Corrupt Slime
Nazar	Dropped from Enchanted Sword, Cursed Hammer, Crimson Axe or Cursed Sku
Megaphone	Dropped from green jellyfish, Dark Mummy or pixie
Bezoar	Dropped from Toxic Sludge, Moss Hornet or hornet
Adhesive Bandage	Dropped from Rusty Armored Bones, angler fish or werewolf

TERRA BLADE

If you thought crafting Night's Edge was a challenge, you ain't seen nothing yet! The Terra Blade is one of the most powerful weapons in the game, and you'll even get a special entr in your Steam account's Achievements page to celebrate your first time crafting it!

SHOPPING LIST

Remember Night's Edge? The Wizard told you to hold on to it until Hardmode for a good reason ... You're about to put it to good use again!

ITEM	WHERE TO FIND IT
Night's Edge	See Night's Edge section on page 39
Hallowed Bar (12)	Dropped by the Twins, the Destroyer, or Skeletron Prime
Broken Hero Sword (2)	Dropped by Mothron during solar eclipse

CRAFTING THE ANKH SHIELD

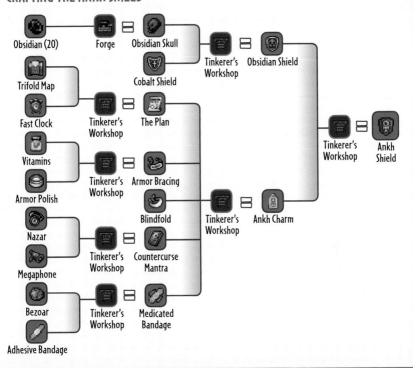

CRAFTING THE TERRA BLADE

Your main difficulty in crafting the Terra Blade will be acquiring two **Broken Hero Swords**. These drop from **Mothron**, a challenging mini-boss that appears during the solar eclipse once you have defeated all three Mechanical Bosses (the Twins, the Destroyer and Skeletron Prime).

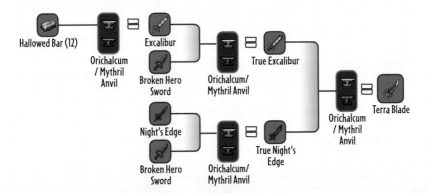

🦂 CELL PHONE

A true wonder of goblin engineering, the cell phone is not only one of the most useful items in the game, but it's also the most complex to craft. Not only does the cell phone return you home when you use it, but it can also display tons of useful info, ranging from the phase of the moon to whether there are rare enemies nearby.

SHOPPING LIST

You'll have to be incredibly patient to assemble all the items required to craft a cell phone. Some of them are rare drops, while others must be acquired through fishing quests. Just keep an eye open for the items you need!

ITEM		WHERE TO FIND IT
🪙 🪙	Gold/Platinum Bar (10)	Crafted from Gold/Platinum Ore
⚙️ ⚙️	Magic Mirror or Ice Mirror	Chests (Underground, Cavern, or Underground Jungle)
🔗	Chain	Crafted from Iron/Lead Bar
🧭	Compass	Drops from salamanders, Giant Shellys, crawdads, Mother Slimes, Snow Flinxes, Undead Vikings, or Dead Vikings
📟	Depth Meter	Drops from cave bats, salamanders, giant bats, Giant Shellys, jungle bats, or Ice Bats
📘	Fisherman's Pocket Guide	Rewards from fishing quest
📻	Weather Radio	
📐	Sextant	
🗡️	Metal Detector	Drops from nymphs
⏱️	Stopwatch	Sometimes sold by Traveling Merchant
📟	DPS Meter	
📖	Lifeform Analyzer	
📟	Tally Counter	Drops from Angry Bones, Cursed Skulls, or Dark Casters
📟	Radar	Wooden Chests (Surface) / Wooden Crates (from fishing)

WELL DONE, MASTER CRAFTSMAN!

Now that I've shared all my goblin crafting secrets with you, you're well on your way to becoming a true crafting master! But where should you put all these amazing tools, weapons, blocks and pieces of furniture?

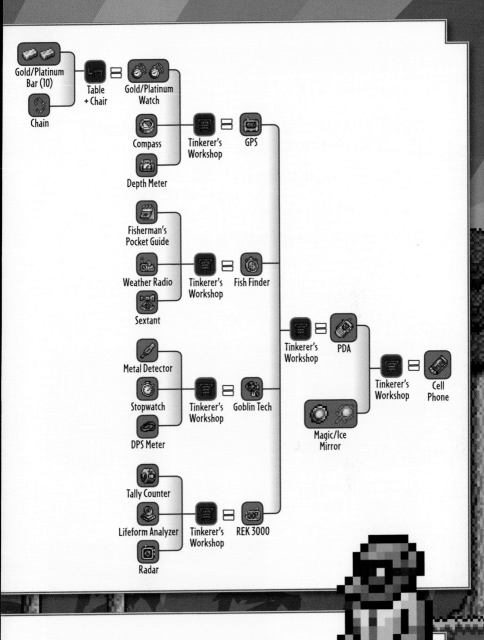

Gold/Platinum Bar (10) · **Table + Chair** = **Gold/Platinum Watch**

Chain

Compass · **Depth Meter** → **Tinkerer's Workshop** = **GPS**

Fisherman's Pocket Guide · **Weather Radio** · **Sextant** → **Tinkerer's Workshop** = **Fish Finder**

Metal Detector · **Stopwatch** · **DPS Meter** → **Tinkerer's Workshop** = **Goblin Tech**

Tally Counter · **Lifeform Analyzer** · **Radar** → **Tinkerer's Workshop** = **REK 3000**

Tinkerer's Workshop = **PDA**

Tinkerer's Workshop = **Cell Phone**

Magic/Ice Mirror

Want to build a vampire castle? How about a spaceship or a massive underground base? That's the beauty of Terraria: YOU decide!

43

CHAPTER FIVE:
CONSTRUCTION BASICS

THE FOUNDATIONS OF SOUND CONSTRUCTION

Building in Terraria is pretty simple, but it offers infinite possibilities. Here is a refresher, plus some new Tinkerer tips and tricks, that will make it easier to create your architectural wonder.

BUILDING CONTROLS

To place a brick, wall, platform or object, simply select the item you want to place and check your mouse pointer. You can only place objects near you; if your cursor turns back into the normal pointer, you're out of range.

Red squares on the object mean something's blocking the way.

Blocked! The staircase is preventing placement.

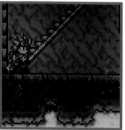
Out of range! Better get closer.

There. Perfect!

BUILD STRAIGHT FROM THE INVENTORY

To save time on construction projects, you can simply click on an item in your inventory and place it in the environment. This only works when **Autopause** is off in the Settings menu.

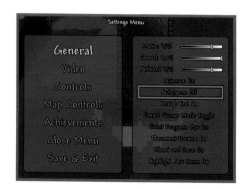

EFT, RIGHT, LEFT, RIGHT

When placing items like
chairs, the direction they
face depends on your own
orientation. Turn left or
right to change your item's
direction when placing it.

ANOTHER BRICK IN THE WALL

Walls not only look good, but they also prevent monsters from appearing inside your
buildings. You can place them by selecting a wall in your inventory or Hotbar and
clicking on the background. You can destroy background walls with the **hammer**.

If you want to place walls
directly below the ground,
you'll need to first destroy the
Dirt Wall using your hammer,
starting from one of the edges.
The natural walls disappear
further down.

Clearing a Dirt Wall with the hammer

SLIPPERY SLOPE

You can also use the hammer to create slopes. Select the hammer
and click on a block to change its slope. Click a total of five times to
return the block to its initial state.

FLOATING BUILDINGS

While you can only place blocks next to existing ones, there's no need to keep your constructions earthbound! Here's a Tinkerer tip: to create floating structures, start building from the ground or an existing construction, then simply remove the linking blocks.

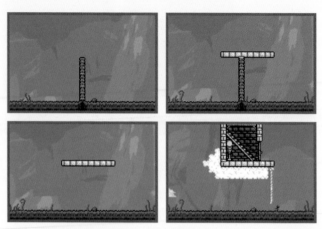

Not really a floating tower ... More like a tower that forgot to fall!

WORK SMARTER, NOT HARDER

You can turn **Smart Cursor** on or off by pressing the **Left Control** key. This makes building a lot easier, but be careful to turn it off if you want to place or destroy a specific block.

SELECTED TOOL	EFFECT
Pickaxe	Mines a passage in the direction of your cursor
Axe	Chops the base of the tree or cactus nearest to the cursor
Hammer	Removes the wall nearest to the cursor
Block	Places a block nearest to the cursor
Wall	Places a wall nearest to the cursor
Platform	Extends an existing platform towards the cursor (creates staircase if cursor is diagonal)
Acorn	Plants an acorn on a free spot
Minecart Track	Extends existing track
Wrench	Extends existing wire
Wire Cutter	Removes wire
Staff of Regrowth	Plants grass or moss nearest to the cursor

Placing walls using Smart Cursor

BUILDING A BEDROOM

Using a **bed** and a bedroom, you can set your **spawn point**, the location you'll return to when you load the game, use a Magic Mirror, Ice Mirror or cell phone, or when you die.

WHAT MAKES A BEDROOM?

If your bedroom is big enough, has walls, a ceiling and a floor, and has a background wall and a bed, then you're good to go! Natural walls such as underground dirt don't count, though; you'll have to set your own wall.

To set your spawn point, right-click on the bed. Right-click again to reset it.

A small bedroom

SURVIVAL TIP

Considering how often I bring you back from the brink of death, why not place your bed directly in my house? Next time you're about to expire from poison or a lava burn, you can just teleport home for a quick heal!

MAKE YOUR BED

There are twenty-six types of beds that you can craft, as well as five that can only be found. The bed styles are a simple matter of look: the basic bed does the job just as well as the fancier ones.

RECIPE	INGREDIENTS	CRAFTING STATION
Bed (1)	Wood (15) Silk (5)	Sawmill

ALLY HOUSES

The key to attracting allies is to build houses for us. Much like bedrooms, houses have special requirements.

WHAT MAKES A HOUSE

A building has to be big enough to be considered a house. It must also feature a **flat surface**, a **chair**, a **door** and a **light source**.

A minimalist house

Minimum house sizes

THE HOUSING QUERY

An easy way to verify if a construction can work as a house is to use the **Housing Query**. From the Inventory menu, click on the **Housing** button on the right. Select the **Query** option and click on the house you want to check.

Housing Menu   Housing Query

ASSIGNING ALLIES

We allies will move on our own into available houses. However, if you want to decide who should go where, you just have to click a portrait in the **Housing menu**, then click on the house you want. When a house is assigned to an ally, you'll see their portrait on the wall.

Want to evict one of us? Just right-click on our portrait!

A house fit for a wizard

CONSTRUCTION TOOLS

A goblin builder is only as good as his or her tools. The following items are not absolutely necessary for building, but they certainly make construction projects a whole lot easier. Many of them are sold by the Traveling Merchant, but he won't always have them in stock. Be sure to check out his wares whenever he's around!

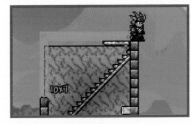

Using the ruler

ITEM		USE	HOW TO GET IT
	Mechanical Ruler	Displays transparent grid	Sold by Mechanic
	Ruler	Displays measurement tool	Sold by Goblin Tinkerer
	Toolbelt	Block placement range +1	
	Toolbox	Item placement and tool range +1	Found in presents at Christmas
	Paint Sprayer	Automatically paints placed objects	
	Extendo Grip	Tile reach +3	Sold by Traveling Merchant
	Portable Cement Mixer	Wall placement speed increased	
	Brick Layer	Tile placement speed increased	

HELPFUL HACK

Can't wait for Christmas to get the toolbox? Trick Father Christmas by changing the date on your computer! Just make sure to set it back once you're done.

THE ARCHITECT GIZMO PACK

Here's a neat goblin trick to save inventory space: combine the functionality of all these four tools into the **Architect Gizmo Pack**.

RECIPE	INGREDIENTS	CRAFTING STATION
Architect Gizmo Pack	Brick Layer (1) Extendo Grip (1) Paint Sprayer (1) Portable Cement Mixer (1)	Tinkerer's Workshop

CAMERA MODE

What good is it to build architectural wonders if you can't show off to your friends? Fortunately, Terraria offers a few ways to capture your buildings in all their glory.

SELFIE TIME!

To access Camera mode, either press **F1** or click the **Camera mode** button on the top right of the inventory screen.

This will replace your inventory with the Camera mode interface.

FUNCTION	DESCRIPTION
Take Screenshot	Captures the entire screen
Take Snapshot	Captures the content within the frame
Pin Frame	Defines the frame using left and right mouse buttons
Set Frame	Fixes the frame for a snapshot
Reset Frame	Removes the frame
Open Map	Opens the map in Camera mode
Settings	Opens the Settings menu
Open Folder	Opens the folder containing your images (Can only be used in Windowed mode)
Close	Closes the Camera mode interface

USING THE FRAME

If you want to take a picture of the whole screen, just click **Take Screenshot**. Otherwise, you can set a frame by clicking **Pin Frame**. Next, click the left and right buttons of your mouse to set the corners of your frame.

Once you're happy with the Frame, click **Set Frame**, then **Take Snapshot**. Say 'Rocket Boots!'

Setting a frame

USING THE MAP

By clicking on the **Open Map** button or by pressing **'M'**, you can set a frame using the map instead of the screen.

If **Image Packing** is selected in the Settings menu, taking a snapshot will scale down everything to fit into a single image. Otherwise, the game will cut up the screenshot into different full-size pictures.

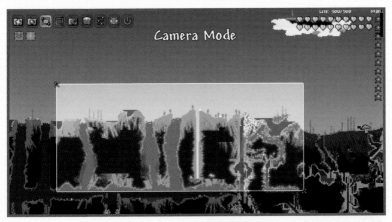

Using the map inside Camera mode

SETTINGS

The Settings panel lets you tweak the way you capture images. From here, you can hide your character, allies, monsters and pets from snapshots, hide the background, or change the background type.

HELPFUL HACK

By default, Terraria saves your screenshots in **Documents/My Games/Terraria/Captures**. While the game is in a window instead of full screen (that is, in 'Windowed mode'), you can access the folder with the **Open Folder** button. To switch between Windowed mode and full screen, press **Alt + Enter**.

CHAPTER SIX: WIRES AND TRACKS

ADVANCED CONSTRUCTION TOOLS

Wiring and tracks are powerful construction tools that open up a lot of really cool possibilities. Let's get you on track and wired up!

WIRING BASICS

To gain access to wiring tools, you'll first need to rescue my favourite human, the **Mechanic**, from the Dungeon. Once you free her, she'll move into an available house and will sell you everything you need.

But I was almost done putting blinking lights up here!

DOWN THE WIRE: BASIC WIRING

You can connect a **trigger** to a **triggered object** using **wire**. To do so, select the **wrench** and click to place wire. Make sure the wire runs uninterrupted between the two and that both ends touch the trigger and the object, and you've got a circuit. Simple!

WIRING TIP

Wires only appear when you have selected a wiring-related item such as a **wrench**, a **wire cutter** or any kind of trigger. Use this to your advantage to spot the wires used to trigger underground traps!

WIRE COLOURS

The Mechanic sells three different coloured wrenches. Using all three, you can create overlapping circuits that won't interfere with one another.

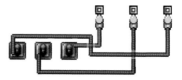

These three circuits work independently, despite crossed wires

WIRING TRIGGERS

You can use many different items to trigger your circuits. Here are some of them.

SWITCHED ON: LEVERS AND SWITCHES

Levers and switches serve the same purpose; the only difference between them is size and appearance. Both can be placed on the ground or on a background wall. You can trigger them by right-clicking on them.

Wall-mounted switch (left) and lever (right)

UNDER PRESSURE: PRESSURE PLATES

Pressure plates trigger circuits when stepped on. The way to trigger them depends on their type:

TYPE	TRIGGERED BY
Gray Pressure Plate	
Brown Pressure Plate	
Blue Pressure Plate	Players only
Lihzahrd Pressure Plate	
Red Pressure Plate	Players, allies and monsters
Green Pressure Plate	
Yellow Pressure Plate	Allies and monsters
Pressure Plate Track	Minecarts

TIME IS ON MY SIDE: TIMERS

When activated, **timers** will trigger a connected circuit at regular intervals. To activate a timer, right-click on it. You can even trigger them through a separate circuit!

RECIPE	INGREDIENTS	CRAFTING STATION
1 Second Timer (1)	Gold/Platinum Watch (1) Wire (1)	
3 Second Timer (1)	Silver/Tungsten Watch (1) Wire (1)	Iron/Lead Anvil
5 Second Timer (1)	Copper/Tin Watch (1) Wire (1)	

INTERNET TIP

One second is not fast enough for you? Some clever Terraria players have created crazy machines that can trigger circuits much faster. Look on the Official Wiki for **Bird Engine** and **Crab Engine**.

TRIGGERING OBJECTS

In addition to **lights**, **doors** and **traps**, you can activate a number of interesting objects using wires. Here are a few ideas!

MEDUSA'S GARDEN: STATUES

Of all the statues you can find, some can be triggered using a circuit. Many Monster Statues will spawn a monster, which can be useful when you're hunting for a particular item.

 When triggered, the **Bomb Statue** will generate bombs, while the **Star Statue** and **Heart Statue** will create Stars and Hearts to boost your mana and health.

PUMP IT UP: PUMPS

By connecting an **Inlet Pump** and **Outlet Pump** and wiring them to a trigger, you can transport water, honey or lava across the circuit even over great distances.

The pump system will work as long as the Inlet Pump is submerged and the Outlet Pump is not. Each activation will transport about four tiles' worth of liquid.

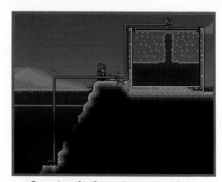

Pumping the Ocean into a seaside aquarium! Why? Why not!

RECIPE	INGREDIENTS	CRAFTING STATION
Inlet Pump (1)	Iron/Lead Bar (10) Wire (2)	Iron/Lead Anvil
Outlet Pump (1)		

IT'S GONNA BLOW: EXPLOSIVES

Explosives are a fun way to clear out space or take out multiple monsters at once. Wire them up with a **Yellow Pressure Plate** and watch the fireworks. Just make sure to stay well away from the area when they're about to go off!

You can buy **dynamite** from the Demolitionist, or find it in chests.

RECIPE	INGREDIENTS	CRAFTING STATION
Explosives (1)	Dynamite (3) Wire (1)	By Hand

BOOM!

PRETTY FLY: TELEPORTERS

The ultimate in long-distance convenience, **teleporters** let you travel between two places in a flash. Just connect two teleporters with wire and a trigger mechanism, and you're good to go. The catch? You'll have to run those wires halfway across the world.

Teleporters can transport players, allies and monsters, so choose your trigger mechanism carefully. For a personal transportation system, use **Gray**, **Brown**, **Blue** or **Lihzahrd Pressure Plates** and place them on top of your teleporter pad!

A teleporter with a Gray Pressure Plate on top

ACTIVE AND INACTIVE STONE BLOCKS

Active Stone Blocks are special blocks that can be turned on and off when triggered. When active, they act as normal Stone Blocks, but when switched off, they will let objects and characters fall through, making them ideal for traps.

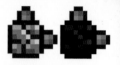

RECIPE	INGREDIENTS	CRAFTING STATION
Active Stone Block (1)	Stone Block (1)	
Inactive Stone Block (1)	Wire (1)	By Hand

A simple lava trap using Active Stone Blocks

ACTUATORS

Actuators function exactly like Active Stone Blocks, except they work with every type of block. Place them over an existing block to allow it to be triggered on and off with wires. The **Mechanic** sells actuators for 10 Silver a piece.

One cool application of actuators is **zombie-proof doors**: place them over a wall, then link them to **Gray Pressure Plates** on either side of the wall. You'll be able to waltz right in, but monsters won't be able to follow!

A zombie-proof door with Blue Pressure Plates

CONSTRUCTION TIP

Keep in mind that actuator-powered walls won't count as a door for the purpose of building houses for your allies.

effort and ingenuity, you can connect every location in your world with your own minecart transit system!

RECIPE	INGREDIENTS	CRAFTING STATION
Minecart Track (50)	Iron/Lead Bar (1) Wood (1)	 Iron/Lead Anvil

TRACK BASICS

You can ride a minecart by right-clicking on a track. If you haven't placed a cart in your Special Equipment tab, you'll ride a wooden minecart by default. To move along the track, press left or right. Pressing in the opposite direction of your travel will let you brake.

To get off the minecart, press **'R'**.

INTERSECTIONS

You can connect minecart tracks together into intersections by hitting the junction point with your hammer. Hitting the intersection again will switch the default direction of the intersection.

Regardless of the default direction, hold **Up** or **Down** while riding your minecart to choose which route you want to take.

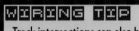

Connecting an intersection, then switching its default direction

WIRING TIP

Track intersections can also be wired! Flip ahead to the 'Wiring Tracks' section on page 59 to find out how.

TERMINUS: TRACK ENDINGS

You can change the end of your tracks by hitting them with the hammer. The **closed** track ending will stop your minecart, while the **bumper** ending will bounce you right back in the other direction. If you run through an **open** track ending, however, you'll fly right off the tracks. Brace yourself for a rough landing!

Closed, bumper and open track endings

THE NEED FOR SPEED: BOOSTER TRACKS

The Mechanic sells **booster tracks**, which can either speed up or slow down your minecart depending on the direction you set them. You can change a booster track's direction by hitting it with the hammer.

Three booster tracks

It will take three booster tracks for a minecart to reach top speed, and five for the mechanical cart to do the same.

CHOOSE YOUR RIDE: MINECARTS

If you find the default wooden minecart too slow, you have some options. The crafted **minecart** and **mechanical cart** are faster carts that you can equip in your Special Equipment page. The mechanical cart is only available on Expert difficulty.

RECIPE	INGREDIENTS	CRAFTING STATION
Minecart (1)	Iron/Lead Bar (15) Wood (10)	Iron/Lead Anvil
Mechanical Cart (1)	Mechanical Wheel Piece (1) Mechanical Wagon Piece (1) Mechanical Battery Piece (1)	Mythril/Orichalcum Anvil

WIRING TRACKS

Many of the elements that make up minecart track systems can be wired for extra functionality and fun. You can switch junctions using various triggers including a pressure plate specifically made for minecarts. Using triggers, you can also reverse the direction of booster tracks.

WIRED JUNCTIONS

By wiring minecart track junctions, you can switch the default direction that carts will take. Switches can happen automatically through pressure plate tracks, or using levers and switches. You can even create your own signalling system by wiring up **Ruby** and **Emerald Gemspark Blocks**!

Lights indicate the default direction of the junction.

PRESSURE PLATE TRACK

Pressure plate tracks are the minecart track equivalent to regular pressure plates. They can only be triggered by a minecart. You can use them to create dynamic junction switch systems.

RECIPE	INGREDIENTS	CRAFTING STATION
Pressure Plate Track (1)	Minecart Track (1) Pressure Plate (1)	Iron/Lead Anvil

One clever use of the pressure plate track is when combined with a **teleporter**. Place your teleporter one block below the pressure plate track and link it to another teleporter for instant long-distance cart travel.

Using teleporters and pressure plate tracks to skip a large body of water

UNLEASH YOUR INNER DECORATOR

This chapter is all style and no substance! Let's talk decoration tips.

BUILDING MATERIALS GUIDE

There are nearly 200 block types in Terraria, including all-natural and crafted block types, and most of them can be crafted into background walls. Check out all the possible building materials below!

NATURAL MATERIALS

These blocks can be gathered from the environment as they are. They are good for creating constructions that have a raw, natural look.

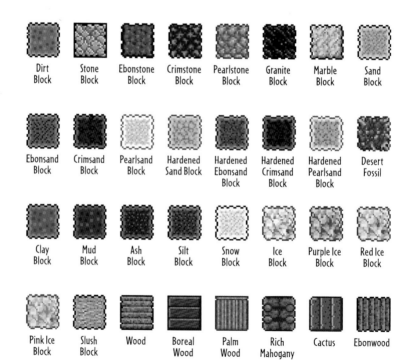

Dirt Block	Stone Block	Ebonstone Block	Crimstone Block	Pearlstone Block	Granite Block	Marble Block	Sand Block
Ebonsand Block	Crimsand Block	Pearlsand Block	Hardened Sand Block	Hardened Ebonsand Block	Hardened Crimsand Block	Hardened Pearlsand Block	Desert Fossil
Clay Block	Mud Block	Ash Block	Silt Block	Snow Block	Ice Block	Purple Ice Block	Red Ice Block
Pink Ice Block	Slush Block	Wood	Boreal Wood	Palm Wood	Rich Mahogany	Cactus	Ebonwood

| Shadewood | Pearlwood | Dynasty Wood | Spooky Wood | Glowing Mushroom | Hay | Pumpkin | Cloud |

| Rain Cloud | Hive | Coralstone Block |

BRICKS

Although it's possible to place ores and bars, converting them into bricks will give your structures a more polished construction feel.

| Gray Brick | Red Brick | Ebonstone Brick | Pearlstone Brick | Sandstone Brick | Snow Brick | Ice Brick | Mudstone Block |

| Iridescent Brick | Copper Brick | Tin Brick | Silver Brick | Tungsten Brick | Gold Brick | Platinum Brick | Demonite Brick |

| Crimtane Brick | Meteorite Brick | Obsidian Brick | Hellstone Brick | Cobalt Brick | Mythril Brick | Chlorophyte Brick | Luminite Brick |

| Rainbow Brick* | Blue Brick | Green Brick | Pink Brick | Lihzahrd Brick |

* Changes colour over time

BLOCKS

These blocks include some animated ones like the Waterfall Block that will give your constructions a truly unique flair.

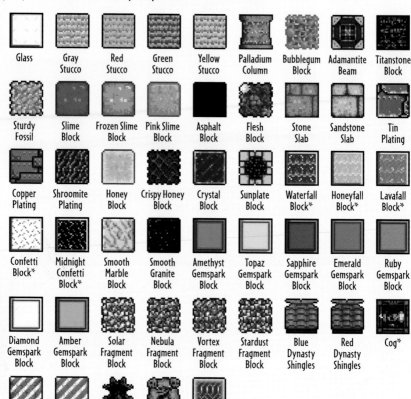

Glass	Gray Stucco	Red Stucco	Green Stucco	Yellow Stucco
Palladium Column	Bubblegum Block	Adamantite Beam	Titanstone Block	
Sturdy Fossil	Slime Block	Frozen Slime Block	Pink Slime Block	Asphalt Block
Flesh Block	Stone Slab	Sandstone Slab	Tin Plating	
Copper Plating	Shroomite Plating	Honey Block	Crispy Honey Block	Crystal Block
Sunplate Block	Waterfall Block*	Honeyfall Block*	Lavafall Block*	
Confetti Block*	Midnight Confetti Block*	Smooth Marble Block	Smooth Granite Block	Amethyst Gemspark Block
Topaz Gemspark Block	Sapphire Gemspark Block	Emerald Gemspark Block	Ruby Gemspark Block	
Diamond Gemspark Block	Amber Gemspark Block	Solar Fragment Block	Nebula Fragment Block	Vortex Fragment Block
Stardust Fragment Block	Blue Dynasty Shingles	Red Dynasty Shingles	Cog*	
Candy Cane Block**	Green Candy Cane Block**	Pine Tree Block**	Bone Block	Martian Conduit Plating

* Animated blocks
** Available at Christmas

BACKGROUND BLOCKS

These special blocks work like furniture: they are placed in the background and will not block your movement. All of them are animated, and the Bubble can even hold liquids.

Living Fire Block	Living Cursed Fire Block	Living Demon Fire Block	Living Frost Fire Block	Living Ichor Fire Block	Living Ultrabright Fire Block	Smoke Block	Bubble

FURNITURE GUIDE

Terraria has tons of furniture you can use to decorate your homes. Some, like the Work Bench, table, or bookcase have useful functions, but many others are just for fun. Use them to give your buildings a homey feel!

FURNITURE TYPES

The following types of furniture pieces all come in many variations to fit with your building theme:

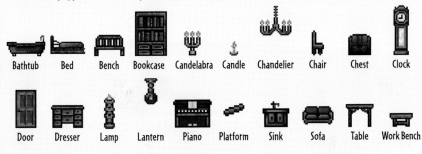

Bathtub	Bed	Bench	Bookcase	Candelabra	Candle	Chandelier	Chair	Chest	Clock

Door	Dresser	Lamp	Lantern	Piano	Platform	Sink	Sofa	Table	Work Bench

FURNITURE SETS

Furniture items come in sets or themes. Many themes correspond to block and wall styles, so it's easy to build something with a particular look and feel.

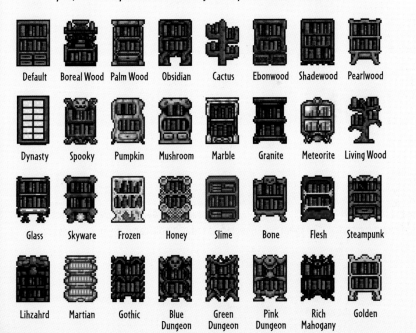

Default	Boreal Wood	Palm Wood	Obsidian	Cactus	Ebonwood	Shadewood	Pearlwood

| Dynasty | Spooky | Pumpkin | Mushroom | Marble | Granite | Meteorite | Living Wood |

| Glass | Skyware | Frozen | Honey | Slime | Bone | Flesh | Steampunk |

| Lihzahrd | Martian | Gothic | Blue Dungeon | Green Dungeon | Pink Dungeon | Rich Mahogany | Golden |

PAINTS

Paints are another great way to customize your constructions. Using a **paintbrush** you can paint any object, brick or block, while a **paint roller** will let you colour background walls. To use them, select them with paint in your inventory; you will automatically use the first colour in your inventory, starting from the top left.

The Painter also sells a **paint scraper** that you can use to remove the colour from any object or wall. The Traveling Merchant sometimes sells a **paint sprayer**, which will automatically paint objects and bricks as you place them.

PAINTING TIP

Once you start crafting **Spectre Bars**, you'll be able to upgrade your painting tools with versions that extend your range by three tiles.

COLOUR INDEX

You can choose from thirty paint hues. All of them except the 'Deep' colours are sold by the Painter. To create the 'Deep' versions, combine two of the same colours at a **Dye Vat**.

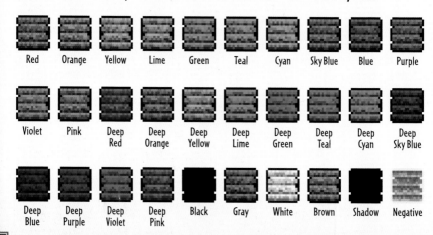

Red · Orange · Yellow · Lime · Green · Teal · Cyan · Sky Blue · Blue · Purple

Violet · Pink · Deep Red · Deep Orange · Deep Yellow · Deep Lime · Deep Green · Deep Teal · Deep Cyan · Deep Sky Blue

Deep Blue · Deep Purple · Deep Violet · Deep Pink · Black · Gray · White · Brown · Shadow · Negative

STYLE TIPS

Creating outstanding buildings requires patience and creativity. Don't be afraid to experiment and break a few rules! Keep screenshots of your work so you can track your progress and share them with friends for comments and ideas.

AVOID BOXES

Slopes and angled rooms break the monotony and create more interesting shapes. Don't settle for simple boxes for your rooms - why not put the walls at an angle and see what happens?

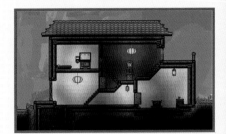

Rooms with an asymmetric design look more intriguing at first glance.

This underground shop blends in with the tunnel's natural look.

USE THE ENVIRONMENT

Take advantage of the natural formations around you when designing your buildings. Want to build a house in a Snow biome? Ice castles and igloos make very memorable buildings!

PICK A THEME

Do you want to build a science-fiction spaceship or a horror-movie castle? How about a giant mushroom or a house in the roots of a giant tree? Whatever you want, use blocks, walls and furniture that work within that theme. Use objects, blocks and painted objects that reinforce your selected style.

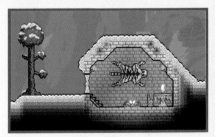

A cool place to chill

CREATE DEPTH

Terraria might be a 2-D world, but you can use some perspective tricks to create a sense of depth for your buildings. Use background walls, angled blocks and paint colours to your advantage.

In this example, by using a background wall to create a pillar and by removing platforms as if they were behind that pillar, you can create the illusion that the staircase spirals upward.

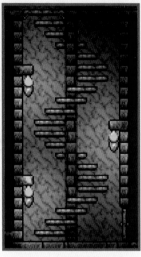

Up and around we go!

THE DEVIL'S IN THE DETAILS

With clever use of furniture, colours and objects, you can make your structures appear full of life. Even small structures can be made exciting by using furniture and other objects in creative and fun ways. While it's fun to create megastructures, bigger isn't always better!

In this example, Wood Platforms allow the placement of objects on top of the fireplace and on the windowsill. The window is made of Glass Walls, and the curtains are Pumpkin Walls painted brown. The chimney is a simple Gray Brick Wall placed in line with the fireplace.

Tiny can be cosy.

CHAPTER EIGHT:
CONSTRUCTION IDEAS

RAW INSPIRATION FOR YOUR NEXT BUILDING PROJECT

Need a few good ideas to get your creative juices flowing? Here are a few useful – or just plain cool – projects you can tackle.

CASTLE BASE

Castles are a popular choice for Terraria building, and with good reason – not only do they look cool, but it's also great to build a well-defended base that can withstand even the mighty Goblin Army!

What kind of castle do you want to build? Perhaps a vampire castle with tall gothic spires? Or how about a giant sandcastle . . . or an ice palace?

Welcome to Cloud Princess Castle!

One way to personalize your castle is to use a single theme for your external walls, then create variations for each of your allies' rooms. You can have fun creating cool-looking rooms such as a kitchen, dining hall or even a macabre dungeon!

VILLAGE

You might be tempted to build all our houses inside a single structure like a castle, but why not give us individual homes instead? This way you can really bring out our individual personalities in each building. Shouldn't the Nurse have a whole medical clinic all by herself? What about a goblin forge for me, or a gun shop for the Arms Dealer?

One word of warning: villages are great to visit, but they can spell trouble for us allies when events like the Blood Moon or the Pirate Invasion take place. If you'd rather keep all of us in one place, it might be worth going for a castle-like base instead.

Back already? Did you shoot yourself in the foot again?

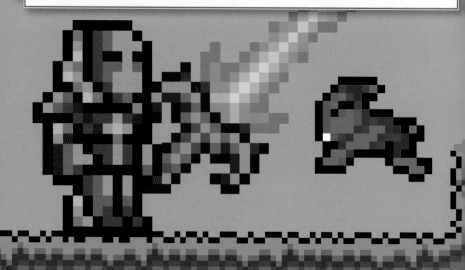

TREE HOUSE

If your world features one or more gigantic trees called Living Trees, you have an opportunity to create a truly unique-looking base for your allies. Using the Living Trees' natural shapes, you can dig a series of rooms and customize them based on each resident's skills and personality.

Be careful with the Living Leaf and Living Wood Blocks, as they are hard to replace if you mine them by mistake. Look in the roots of the Living Tree for three useful items: the **Living Wood Wand**, the **Leaf Wand** and the **Living Loom**. The wands let you recreate the Living Trees' unique blocks, while the Living Loom allows you to craft the Living Wood furniture set.

HELPFUL HACK

Not all worlds contain Living Trees, and not all Living Trees have the above tools. If you can't find what you're looking for, create a new world and look again!

BOSS BATTLE ARENA

A good arena makes the difference between victory and death when battling bosses. The ideal arena has plenty of space to move around and lets you jump up and down platforms to dodge boss attacks.

Whenever you find **Heart Statues** and **Star Statues** underground, place them around your arena and wire them to a **5 Second Timer** to get a steady supply of health and mana in battle. **Campfires** and **Heart Lanterns** are also great. Finally, you should consider placing a house for the Nurse nearby for when you need a healing in a hurry.

Your arena can be minimalist if you want, but you can also have fun with it. Why not include viewing platforms or an announcer's box? They'll make your boss battles even more entertaining!

COMBAT TIP

For events that feature tons of invading enemies such as the **Goblin Invasion** or the **Blood Moon**, you can build a separate arena filled with traps and lava pits. Use them to kill massive numbers of monsters at once!

HELLEVATOR

Once you start mining Obsidian and Hellstone, it's a good idea to dig a hole straight down to the Underworld. Terraria players have taken to calling this a 'Hellevator'.

Creating your own Hellevator is a dangerous endeavour, even for a goblin. You'll most likely encounter water and lava on the way down: make sure to redirect water to avoid drowning, and be careful not to flood your tunnels with lava!

To dig down through lava, fill your tunnel with water. Just remember to go up for air!

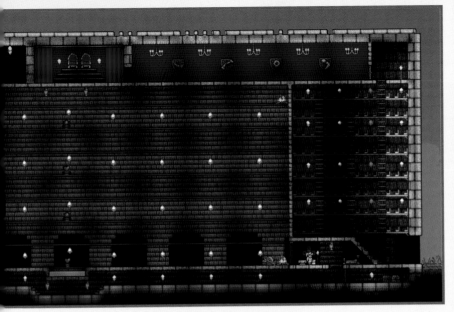

A boss battle arena with a Nurse station at the bottom right

While a simple hole will do the trick, you can take some time to make your Hellevator look nice. Because if you're going to Hell, why not do it in style?

A wide Hellevator with depth marker

MASS-TRANSIT SYSTEM

One of the most useful construction projects you can undertake is a mass-transit system. This will let you move around quickly and safely between locations as you gather resources and progress in the game.

SKY BRIDGE

A Sky Bridge is a great way to get around your world. Build a tower high up above the ground, then place a path going left and right as far as you can. This will take a lot of material to make, but it will save you tons of time getting around. Just be sure not to put it too high in space, to avoid attracting **harpies**.

Just a simple Stone Block platform will do the trick, but it's more fun to build actual station stops along the way. You can place minecart tracks to speed up your movement, or if you have the Blend-O-Matic, it will allow you to create Asphalt Blocks that'll take you everywhere in a jiffy. Consider placing signs at various points of interest along your Sky Bridge so you know where to get off!

It's a good idea to place solid blocks under your track and a platform on top. This way, **Fallen Stars** will fall right on to your Sky Bridge, making it super easy to collect them. Unfortunately, your bridge will also block meteor strikes! One solution is to place actuators on the floor and wire everything to a lever, so you can deactivate your bridge when you're not using it to collect Fallen Stars.

Dungeon station! Next stop: the Ocean!

TUBE STATIONS

There's no need to keep your mass-transit network above ground, either! You can connect interesting underground locations with a vast network of minecart tracks. While you're at it, why not turn it into a fully fledged transit system? Imagine riding the tube from the Ocean to the Underground or the Corruption, each with its own modern-looking station!

Mind the gap!

By using **Minecart Pressure Plates**, you can create routes that use common segments of rails and switch dynamically depending on the direction you're coming from. You can even turn your Sky Bridge into one line of your underground system to make your transport network truly useful.

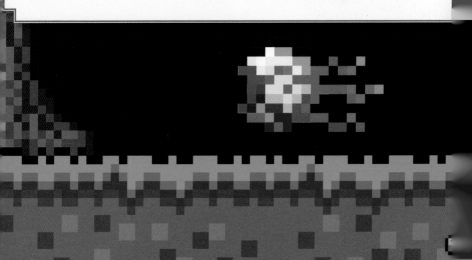

TELEPORTER NETWORK

Riding around the world in a minecart may be exhilarating, but for sheer convenience nothing beats the teleporter. There's no maximum range as long as your teleporters are wired together, so you can literally travel across the world in an instant.

The hard work here is to run wires all the way across the world the first time, but once that's done, you're all set. Great locations for wiring a teleporter include the Dungeon, the Underworld and the Underground Jungle.

Make sure to gather all your teleporter pads in one location near your home base for ultimate convenience.

Where do you want to go today?

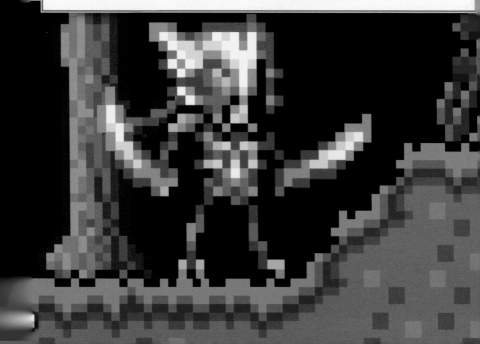

CHAPTER NINE: MEET THE MASTERS

A SHOWCASE OF THE TERRARIA COMMUNITY

Terraria has attracted some incredibly creative and imaginative players over the years. Here are just a few examples of their amazing work.

THRONE ROOM BY OVISARIESBOMBUS

One creative way to use coloured blocks and walls is as pixels in vast works of art. OvisAriesBombus's throne room is a great example: it uses painted glass to create a truly majestic homage to the Moon Lord and the Celestial Towers. Check out also the large bell in the tower to the far right!

FLYING CASTLE BY DRAZELIC

Massive and stylish, Drazelic's unique flying base combines pixel art and cool, functional design into something truly original and epic. The ringed planet logo at the top would make even a goblin master proud.

BLACKJACK MACHINE BY DICEMANX

We goblins know a thing or two about mechanics, but when I look at this creation even I can only stare in disbelief. Using a system that pushes Terraria to its limits, DicemanX has created a functioning blackjack machine. Yes, you read this right: you can actually play blackjack using Terraria physics as the computer!

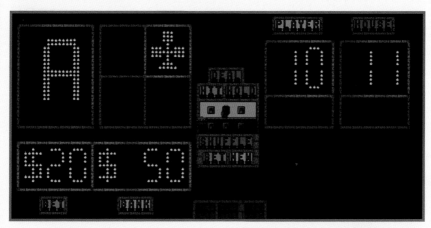

The game is controlled by the three levers in the middle of the screenshot.

DicemanX uses a number of tricks, glitches and exploits known as 'Hoiktronics', the extent of which is enough to make a poor goblin's head explode.

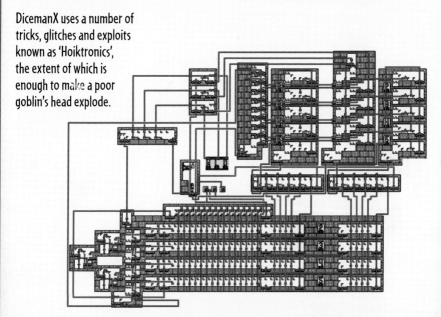

A peek at the schematics of DicemanX's blackjack engine

ARABIAN CITY BY FLORS

There's so much to love in this city design, from the elegance of its oriental domes to the dreamy quality of its ships in the harbour. Flors' construction is proof that picking an original theme and sticking to it can really pay off to create something memorable.

Flors makes great use of curves and inclines, whether in the angles of the ship's sails or the curved domes themselves. Can't you almost smell the spices from here?

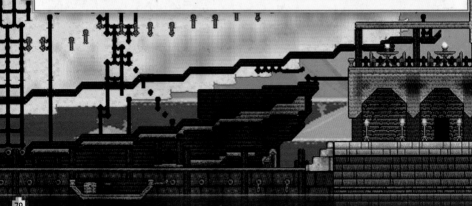

ROOM DESIGN BY BRUSHSTROKE

Some creations are breathtaking in scale while others shine with their attention to detail. In the case of BrushStroke, it's both at the same time: his base is vast, yet every single room is filled with fantastic little creative touches that make it come alive.

BrushStroke's rooms include a pirate's den, a kitchen, a bar and even a pool.

Pirate's den

Well-stocked kitchen

CONGRATULATIONS, MASTER BUILDER!

Now that I have passed my expert knowledge on to you, you have all the tools you need to join Terraria's elite architects! It's time to explore on your own and bring new wonders to life.

Even my goblin craftsmanship is nothing compared to the creations of Terraria players like you. Every day, you humans discover crazy new ways to turn raw resources into cool-looking or awe-inspiring buildings. Many of the ideas I've shown you in this book were inspired by members of the Terraria community just like you.

Remember: be patient, try new things, and take plenty of screenshots to show to your friends or share online. Most importantly, have fun!

MORE CRAFTING AND CONSTRUCTION INSPIRATION

Check out these websites for more crafting and building help and ideas!

OFFICIAL WEBSITE
www.terraria.org

FACEBOOK PAGE
www.facebook.com/TerrariaOfficial

TWITTER ACCOUNT
www.twitter.com/Terraria_Logic

COMMUNITY FORUMS
forums.terraria.org

OFFICIAL TERRARIA WIKI
terraria.gamepedia.com

TERRARIA ON REDDIT*
www.reddit.com/r/terraria
www.reddit.com/r/TerrariaDesign

TERRARIA WIKIA*
terraria.wikia.com

* Websites not monitored by Re-Logic. Enter at your own risk!